DEC 3 0 2005

P9-ELR-476

What on Earth? Volcanoes

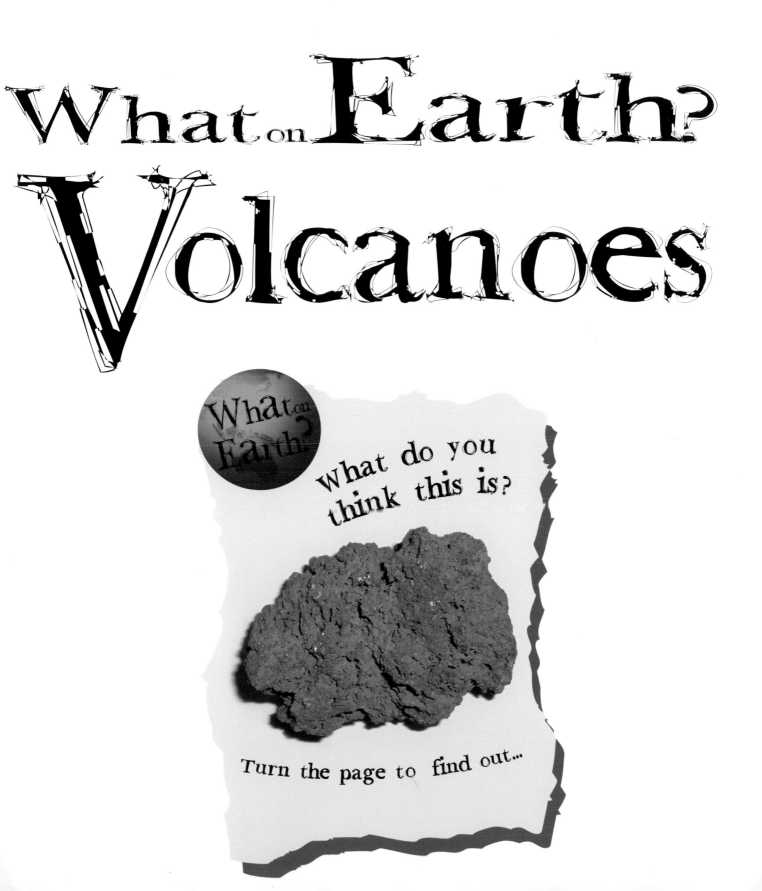

What on Earth?

What do you think this is?

Turn the page to find out...

Published in 2005 in the United States by Children's Press,
an imprint of Scholastic Library Publishing,
90 Sherman Turnpike, Danbury, CT 06816

© **The Salariya Book Company Ltd MMV**

ISBN 0-516-25324-7 (Lib. Bdg)

A CIP catalogue record for this title is available now from the Library of Congress.

Printed and bound in China.

Editors:	Ronald Coleman
	Sophie Izod
Senior Art Editor:	Carolyn Franklin
DTP Designer:	Mark Williams

Picture Credits Dave Antram: 8(b), 14(l), 15, 19(t,), 22,
23(m), 24, 25(t), Julian Baker & Janet Baker (J B
Illustrations): 8(t), 9(t), Mark Bergin: 2, 18, 19(b), 19(t),
Elizabeth Branch: 20-21, 24(t), Peter Bull: 16(r), 17(l), Ray
and Corinne Burrows: 14(b), 16(l), Nick Hewetson: 6-7, 12,
23, 25(b), Tony Townsend: 16-17, 26, Jim Sugar /Corbis: 28,
Digital Stock: 9, 23, PhotoDisc: 11, 13, The Salariya Book
Company: 1, 31

Cover © Jim Sugar/Corbis Images

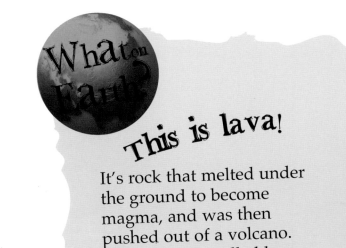

What on Earth?

This is lava!

It's rock that melted under the ground to become magma, and was then pushed out of a volcano. After that, it's called lava.

Careful! It's sharp!

What on Earth? Volcanoes

KATHRYN SENIOR

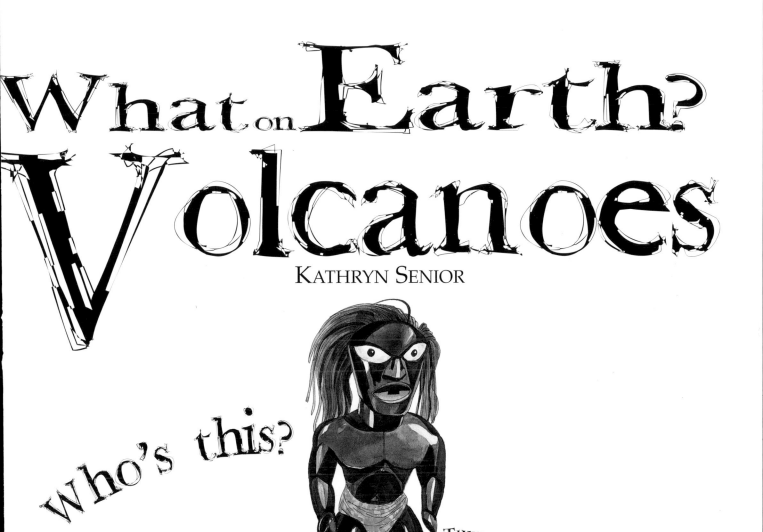

Who's this?

Turn to page 19 to find out!

children's press

A Division of Scholastic Inc.

NEW YORK • TORONTO • LONDON • AUCKLAND • SYDNEY

MEXICO CITY • NEW DELHI • HONG KONG

DANBURY, CONNECTICUT

Contents

What on Earth?

Weird warning!

On May 5, 1902, thousands of snakes invaded the town of St. Pierre in the Caribbean island of Martinique. Three days later the volcano Mount Pelée erupted.

Hisssss

Introduction

 olcanoes form around holes that lead deep below Earth's surface. Every now and then, molten rock, ash, rocks or gases may be forced up through the volcano.

Do all volcanoes look the same?

Many volcanoes look like steep mountains, but some are just cracks in the Earth's surface. Some volcanoes are islands rising out of the sea, and others are on land.

Do volcanoes erupt very often?

Some volcanoes erupt almost all the time. Others may erupt every few years, or maybe not for hundreds or thousands of years. When a volcano is likely to erupt, we say it is active. When it has not erupted for a long time, we say it is dormant. A volcano that has stopped erupting altogether is called extinct.

Why Do Volcanoes Erupt?

Volcanoes erupt because of the way that Earth is made. Beneath the hard outer crust where we live, there is a layer of very hot rock. In places, the rock is so hot that it melts and forces its way up through the crust. This is what is happening when a volcano erupts.

Geyser

What are plate tectonics?

Earth's crust is made up of huge sections called "tectonic plates", floating on a layer of rock. The plates are always moving and sometimes force each other upwards, forming mountain ranges.

Earth's plates, outlined, move in the directions shown by the arrows.

Why are eruptions dangerous?

Molten rock from a volcano is so hot that it burns everything in its path. Many tons of rock, ash and burning gases may explode from the top or side of a volcano spreading death and destruction all around.

What is magma?

Magma is rock that is so hot that it has become a liquid. Sometimes, it collects in large pools called magma chambers. It is lighter than the harder rock around it, and rises upwards towards Earth's crust. When the magma reaches the surface it is called lava.

Lava

Smoke

Magma chamber

What on Earth?

"Old Faithful?"

Yellowstone National Park in the USA is home to "Old Faithful" whose name comes from the regular spurts of hot water and steam which shoot up in the air.

Whoooooosh!

Where Are Volcanoes?

Many of Earth's volcanoes are found along the edges of the tectonic plates that make up Earth's crust, where the crust is weakest. Magma from chambers under the crust forces its way out at these weak points. The maps on these pages show how volcanoes lie in lines along the edges of the tectonic plates.

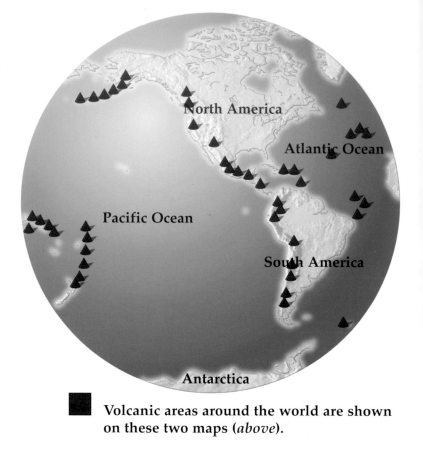

Volcanic areas around the world are shown on these two maps (*above*).

Are there volcanoes near where people live?

Yes, the soil around volcanoes is often very good for growing crops. People start farms and build homes there. There are farms on the slopes of Mount Etna in Italy.

What is the "Pacific Ring of Fire"?

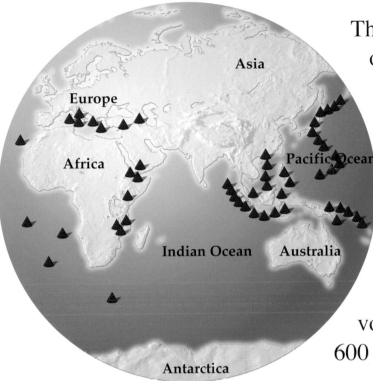

The Pacific Ring of Fire is the ring of volcanoes that surrounds the Pacific Ocean. These volcanoes are all on the edges of a huge tectonic plate. More than half the world's active volcanoes are found here. Indonesia, at the edge of the plate, has 70 active volcanoes – more than any other country! These volcanoes have erupted more than 600 times in the last 200 years.

Where is Mount Fuji?

Mount Fuji is the highest and most sacred mountain in Japan. It is one of the most beautiful mountains in the world. It is a dormant volcano, which last erupted in 1707.

What Happens When a Volcano Erupts?

Eruptions are not always huge explosions. In fact, some are quiet, with thick lava flowing out of the volcano very slowly. If the lava is thin, it is much more dangerous, because it flows faster. Sometimes, lava cools and is thrown out as rocky "bombs".

How can we tell if a volcano will erupt?

It's difficult! Sometimes, a volcano sends out smelly gases. Some volcanoes start to bulge, and then erupt from the side instead of the top. This happened when Mount St. Helens in the USA erupted in 1980.

How long do eruptions last?

Eruptions can be over very quickly – or they may go on for years. Stromboli, in Italy, has been erupting every few minutes for 2,000 years! A volcano stops erupting when there is no more gas or rock to come out of it. It will also stop if the lava cools and makes a plug of rock so nothing more can escape.

Which is the largest active volcano?

Mauna Loa in Hawaii is the world's largest volcano. It is 13,677 feet (4,168 meters) above sea level. Its top is 56,000 feet (17 kilometers) above its base on the ocean floor.

What Kinds of Eruptions Are There?

There are many different kinds of volcanic eruptions. Some volcanoes always erupt in the same way, but others may erupt in different ways at different times. Some eruptions are named after other volcanoes that have erupted in similar ways. The illustration below describes different types of eruptions.

Hawaiian

Hawaiian eruptions, named after Hawaii, are when magma escapes from a crack in Earth's surface, or from a central point.

Pelean

Pelean ("glowing cloud") eruptions are named after Mount Pelée. An explosion of burning gas, dust and ash races down the mountain.

Strombolian

In Strombolian eruptions, huge amounts of molten lava burst from the crater, making sparks in the sky.

Vulcanian
Vulcanian eruptions (named after Vulcano, see page 18) are when gas filled with ash explodes from the crater, forming a cloud near the volcano's top.

Plinian

In Plinian eruptions (named after a Roman writer), thick lava, ash and gas explode high into the air.

What is a shield volcano?

In a shield volcano, lava pours out of one or more vents (cracks) in Earth's crust. Lava flows out in all directions and hardens. Over hundreds of years, this builds up a broad, sloping cone, like a warrior's shield. Mauna Loa in Hawaii is a shield volcano.

Shield volcano
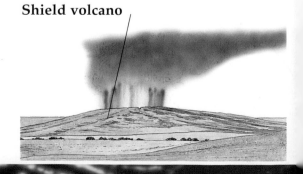

What's the most dangerous eruption?

Pelean eruptions are the most dangerous. Hot, dry rocks and burning gases pour down the mountain very fast. This is called a "pyroclastic flow". One of the most famous eruptions ever was when Mount Vesuvius in Italy erupted in A.D. 79. A pyroclastic flow destroyed three towns: Pompeii, Herculaneum and Stabiae. Many thousands of people died, but we can still see the ruins of the cities today.

What on Earth?

The best place to be?

In 1902, a prisoner in an underground cell was one of only two people to survive when Mount Pelée in Martinique destroyed the town of St. Pierre.

13

Why Are Volcanoes Important?

Volcanoes are very important to us, even though they can cause so much damage. They change the land around them. Sometimes they form new mountains or new islands. Volcanic rocks are full of useful metals, such as copper, silver and gold. They may also contain gemstones, such as diamonds.

What's this?

Vulcanologists use special probes like this to collect samples of lava.

Why do people study volcanoes?

Scientists called "vulcanologists" study volcanoes. They try to find out why and when volcanoes will erupt. This can save many lives.

How do vulcanologists stay safe?

Vulcanologists have to get very close to study volcanoes, and temperatures can reach 1,832 °F (1,000 °C)! This means they must wear protective suits and helmets.

Phew! Wow!

Vulcanologist

Why take photographs?

Filming volcanoes helps scientists study the different kinds of eruptions, and learn more about how people can stay safe.

What on Earth?

Rocks in the bath?

Lava sometimes contains a special kind of rock called pumice. It is very light and very rough. People use it to rub away hard skin from their hands and feet when they take a bath.

Scrub! scrub!

15

How Old Are Volcanoes?

Volcanoes have been around almost as long as planet Earth. The oldest rocks on Earth date from nearly four billion years ago. Scientists studying these can tell that there were volcanoes that long ago. They can also tell how these earthquakes and moving tectonic plates have shaped our world today.

Who put these rocks here?

These rocks in Northern Ireland are called the "Giant's Causeway". There is a legend that a giant put them there. In fact, they formed from lava, around 55-65 million years ago.

Where did this rock come from?

This church in eastern France was built on a volcanic plug. The volcano became extinct and wore away. Only the plug remains.

What happens when tectonic plates move?

Magma bubbles up and escapes through weak places in Earth's crust

Volcanoes erupt where tectonic plates move apart

How do volcanoes change Earth?

New rocks form when lava erupts from volcanoes at the edges of the tectonic plates. In other places, as the plates push against each other, earthquakes occur.

What on Earth?

How did volcanoes kill sea life?

Around 250 million years ago, volcanoes in Siberia pumped out about 10 billion tons of carbon dioxide. This caused global warming. Four-fifths of all sea life died, and it took five million years for Earth to recover.

Lava from volcanoes under the sea hardens and becomes part of Earth's crust

A volcano's vent is like a chimney, leading deep into Earth. Magma travels up through it.

Did We Always Understand Volcanoes?

Today, we have a lot of scientific information about volcanoes. In the past, volcanoes were mysterious and frightening, so people made up stories to explain them. All over the world, there were different myths and legends to explain volcanoes.

What are these crosses?

They are rock crystals formed when Mount Vesuvius erupted in 1660. People thought they were a message from God.

How did volcanoes get their name?

The name "volcano" comes from the Roman god Vulcan. The Romans believed Vulcan was a blacksmith who made weapons for other gods. His forge was under the island of Vulcano near Sicily.

Crash!

Bang!

Bang! Crash! Clang!

How did a warrior become a volcano?

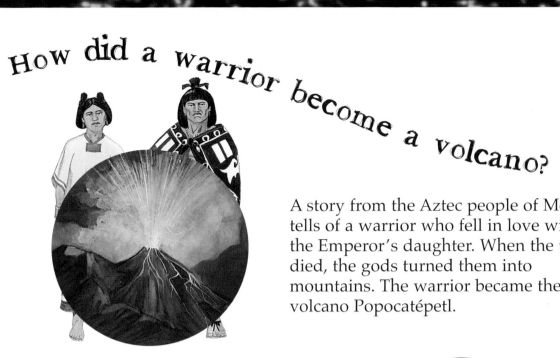

A story from the Aztec people of Mexico tells of a warrior who fell in love with the Emperor's daughter. When the two died, the gods turned them into mountains. The warrior became the volcano Popocatépetl.

Who is Pele?

Pele is the Hawaiian goddess of volcanoes and fire. Hawaiians believe she lives in the volcano Kilauea. Hawaiians tell a story that Pele causes earthquakes by stamping her feet, and makes volcanoes erupt by striking the ground with a stick.

What on Earth?

Who lives on Kilimanjaro?

Kilimanjaro, in Tanzania, is a dormant volcano. It is around 19,000 feet (6,000 meters) above sea level, and is the highest mountain in Africa. No one lives at the snow covered top, but the lower slopes have been home to farmers for thousands of years.

Can Life Come Back?

A big eruption can destroy everything around it. Lava and hot ash burn the plants and kill the animals. However, the land recovers amazingly quickly. After Mount St. Helens in the USA erupted in 1980, everything looked black and dead. But weeks later, tiny insects zoomed in – about two million of them every day. Beetles came to eat the insects, accidentally bringing in plant seeds. Twenty-five years later, the land has almost recovered.

What's special about volcanic soil?

Volcanic soil is very rich in the minerals that plants need to grow well. Where there are many plants, there are also many animals. For example, the beautiful Hawaiian islands were formed from volcanoes. Many kinds of plants grow there, and a large number of animals live among the plants.

Succinea snail

Apapane

What grows first?

Lichens begin to grow on lava after an eruption.

They provide shelter for insects and other small creatures.

Mosses start to grow. Over time, the soil gets thicker and then larger plants grow.

Who hopped in?

Small frogs were among the first animals to live near Mount St. Helens after the eruption. The frogs turned up near mossy pools there, just three years after the lava had cooled.

Hop!

Hop!

Hop!

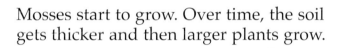

Hawaiian damselfly

Kamehameha butterfly

Hawaiian goose

Iiwi

Can We Tell If a Volcano Is Extinct?

Sometimes it is very hard to tell whether a volcano is extinct (completely dead) or dormant (sleeping). A volcano can appear to be inactive for hundreds or thousands of years, then suddenly burst into action. Even when people are warned of danger, they may not listen. In 1991, Mount Pinatubo in the Philippines had not erupted for 400 years. So when scientists warned people nearby of the danger many did not take any notice. When the eruption came, more than 300 people died.

Why do people get hurt?

Volcanoes can do damage in unexpected ways. When Mount St. Helens erupted in 1980, no one expected the huge mud flows that came down the mountain. Fifty-seven people died in the flows.

Will Mount Fuji erupt?

More than 12 million people live near Mount Fuji in Japan. An eruption could cause huge damage, so the Japanese government is spending millions of dollars to find ways to predict an eruption and protect the people.

Is this volcano dangerous?

Mount Rainier, in northwest USA, is a dormant volcano. An eruption could affect the city of Seattle, which is only about 60 miles (100 kilometers) away.

What on Earth?

What's this?

Devils Tower in Wyoming was once the neck of a volcano that has been eroded (worn away) over many years. It is formed from a steep tower of lava that cooled around 40 million years ago. It is around 1,250 feet (380 meters) tall.

Are There Volcanoes Underwater?

There are around 5,000 active volcanoes under the sea. Some have burst through the surface to become islands. Hawaii is one of these. It is part of a volcanic ridge, formed from a "hot spot" of magma deep underground. It has been pushing through Earth's crust for at least 70 million years.

An underwater vent

What's the Hawaiian Ridge?

The Hawaiian Ridge is a chain of volcanoes in the Pacific Ocean. It is over 1,500 miles (2,400 kilometers) long—the world's longest chain. The Big Island of Hawaii is made up of five shield volcanoes: Kilauea, Mauna Loa, Mauna Kea, Hualalai, and Kohala.

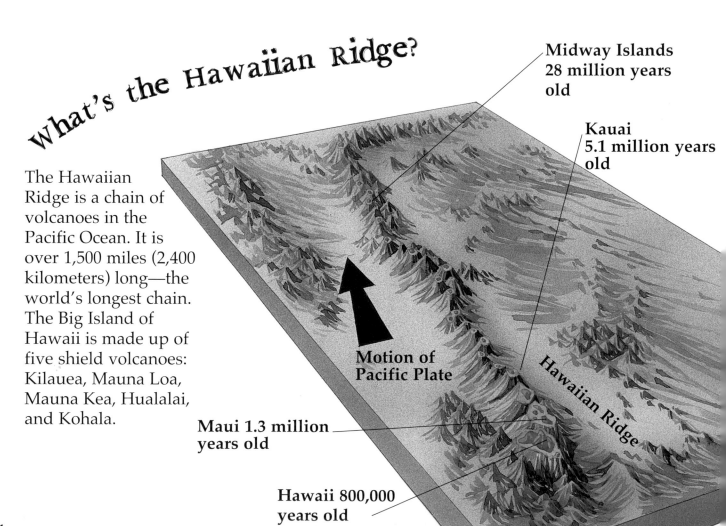

Midway Islands 28 million years old

Kauai 5.1 million years old

Motion of Pacific Plate

Hawaiian Ridge

Maui 1.3 million years old

Hawaii 800,000 years old

What are atolls?

Volcanic island

Coral reef

An atoll is created when a coral reef, made from the skeletons of tiny sea creatures, forms around a volcanic island.

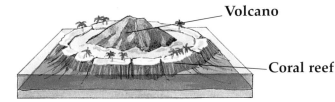

Volcano

Coral reef

After a while, the volcano sinks into the sea. Meanwhile, more coral has formed. In the end, the volcano disappears altogether, but the round coral island remains.

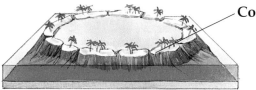

Coral reef

What on Earth Is there hot water under the sea?

There are few living things in the deepest oceans, except near "hydrothermal vents". These are like geysers under the sea. Water, heated by magma under Earth's crust, flows up into the sea.

Mmmm... cozy!

What's a tsunami?

A tsunami is a series of waves caused by an underwater volcanic eruption or earthquake. They can travel in the open sea as fast as 280 miles (450 kilometers) an hour. As they reach the coast they can grow to 100 feet (30 meters) high. A tsunami in Southeast Asia on December 26, 2004, killed over 200,000 people.

Are There Volcanoes on Other Planets?

In our solar system, only Earth and Venus have active volcanoes but there are extinct volcanoes on Mars. Most are on huge domes in regions called Tharsis and Elysium. The Tharsis dome is 2,500 miles (4,000 kilometers) across and 6 miles (10 kilometers) high. It has three large shield volcanoes: Ascraeus Mons, Pavonis Mons and Arsia Mons.

Is this a moon?

Yes it's Io, one of the moons of the planet Jupiter. Its surface is covered with lava flows, lava lakes, giant calderas (collapsed volcanoes) and geysers full of sulphur. Volcanic eruption plumes rise 62 miles (100 kilometers) high.

Volcanic plume

What on Earth?

How many volcanoes does Venus have?

In the 1990s, the Magellan spacecraft found 168 huge volcanoes on Venus, nearly 300 medium-sized ones and hundreds of thousands of smaller ones. Only one, Maat Mons, is definitely active.

How Would You Survive a Volcanic Eruption?

Erupting volcanoes are not the only sign of volcanic activity. The magnificent natural fountains, or geysers, of steam and hot water in the USA, Iceland and New Zealand are all linked to volcanic activity.

Volcano dangers

Burning Lava can reach temperatures of 2,282 °F (1,250 °C) and travel at over 70 mph (113 kph). It's best to get in a car and drive away as quickly as possible!

Being Buried 12 inches (30 cm) of ash is enough to collapse a roof. If possible keep your gutter and roof clear of ash.

Poisoning Store drinking water in bathtubs or containers, as the water supply may become polluted.

What to do checklist

Wear a gas mask because ash can drown you as it mixes with your saliva. Use a pair of goggles to keep you from going blind. Don't leave the house, unless the ash is thick on the roof and it looks like it will collapse. Shut all windows and doors so none of the ash can get inside. Take off outdoor clothing to remove ash and keep a first-aid kit to treat burns.

Other, less dramatic signs are the bubbling pools of hot, thick volcanic mud which often occur near geysers. Smokers are geysers that occur on the seabed, usually where two plates meet.

Volcano Facts

Earth's crust is between 15 miles (25 kilometers) and 47 miles (70 kilometers) thick. Under the oceans, the crust is a lot thinner— only 4 miles (7 kilometers) thick in some places.

It can take years for lava from a volcano to cool. In Mexico, there is a volcano where people can still light sticks of wood from lava that erupted over 40 years ago!

In Japan, there are springs of hot water where monkeys like to bathe in winter to keep warm.

In 1963, scientists in Iceland were able to watch a new island being formed. A volcano erupted under the sea and soon created an island that rose 515 feet (169 meters) above sea level and had an area of nearly 1 square mile (2.5 square kilometers). They called it "Surtsey", after Surtur, the Norse fire giant.

Some volcanoes on Mars are over three billion years old. The youngest ones are about 200 million years old but they are all extinct.

Glossary

active an active volcano is one that could erupt at any time

carbon dioxide a kind of gas

crystal a rock that has formed into a regular shape, such as a square

dormant a dormant volcano is one that has not erupted for a long time, and is not going to do so soon

extinct an extinct volcano will never erupt again

gemstone a jewel stone, such as a diamond

geyser a fountain of natural hot water

hot spot a pocket of magma in Earth's outer layer (its crust)

hydrothermal vent a spring of hot water under the sea

magma rock from deep in Earth's crust that is so hot it has melted

plug magma that has formed a solid block in the center of a volcano

pyroclastic flow hot ash and gas that pours down the side of a volcano

tectonic plate a section of Earth's crust

tsunami a series of huge waves caused by an earthquake or volcano

vent the hole in the center of a volcano

vulcanologist a scientist who studies volcanoes

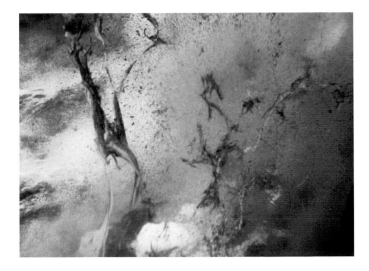

What Do You Know About Volcanoes?

1. What do we call a volcano that will never erupt again?

2. What is magma?

3. Where is the Pacific Ring of Fire?

4. What's a pyroclastic flow?

5. What's a vulcanologist?

6. Who was Vulcan?

7. Where is Popocatépetl?

8. Is Mount Pinatubo in the Philippines extinct?

9. Where's the world's biggest volcano?

10. Besides erupting volcanoes, what's another sign of volcanic activity?

Go to page 32 for the answers!

What is this?

Index

Answers

1. Extinct (See page 5)
2. Rock deep in Earth's crust that is so hot it has become liquid (See page 7)
3. It surrounds the Pacific Ocean (See page 9)
4. Hot, dry rocks and burning gases pouring down a mountain quickly (See page 13)
5. A scientist who studies volcanoes (See page 14)
6. A Roman god believed to be a blacksmith (See page 18)
7. Mexico (See page 19)
8. No (See page 22)
9. Hawaii (See page 11)
10. Natural fountains, or geysers, of steam and hot water (See page 27)

It's a "volcanic bomb", when blobs of lava are thrown out of the volcano. Some solidify in the air, landing as "bombs" on the ground.